Start A Home

By **Amber Richards**

Table of Contents

Introduction

I'd like to share with you a bit about my experiences of operating a home-cleaning business. My hope is that you will benefit from, both, my good and bad business decisions, so that you have the most successful business for your situation. I will be totally transparent in this book about my journey.

I successfully owned and operated an one-person house cleaning service for three years. Ultimately, I had to close my business after that time as I pushed my body beyond its physical limits and developed severe bursitis in my shoulder and I simply couldn't do the work anymore. I could have made other decisions, looking back, but rather, I simply closed my doors, but based on what was happening in my personal life that seemed like the best decision for me at the time.

Why did I start a home cleaning business? I was in a troubled marriage with two young children in elementary school. My husband had just left us, so I was facing single parenthood for the first time. I needed to earn a good income so I wasn't working countless hours away from my children. I needed flexibility in my schedule to accommodate my children's needs. I found that owning my own residential cleaning business fit those criteria best. Because it was also a business, it offered me many tax breaks as well. In that season of my life, it was a great fit for my family and did provide the time, flexibility, and income we needed. Welcome to my journey.

1
Is Self-Employment right for you?

Many are looking for self-employment opportunities in order to support their families financially. For some, there simply may not be jobs available in their areas, while others seek the freedom to set their own hours and pay scale. Whatever the reason, starting your own home cleaning business can be a great solution and a profitable one as well.

However, self-employment is not easy. It takes self-discipline, hard work, meticulous record-keeping, completing different roles and responsibilities, and sometimes delegating certain tasks to others. It also takes wisdom to know the difference between what should be handled by someone else and what should not.

There are many advantages to owning a home-based business. A few are:

1. Flexibility in your schedule

2. Tax credits and savings unique to home-based businesses

3. Having control over how you run your business

4. Providing a valuable service to others

5. Choosing the clients and/or employees you want to work with

6. The rewards of building something from the ground up and seeing it become successful

7. Financial success

It entails handling the proper setup of a business, marketing, and getting new clients, great customer service, a good work ethic, and handling all forms of tax documentation and other necessary paperwork.

Be honest with yourself. There's certainly no shame in doing a personal inventory and realizing that at this stage, it might not fit who you are, your goals right now or that you simply want something easier.

However, don't let these factors scare you off. If you possess the traits above and are willing to work hard and persevere, the rewards can be amazing!

Let me share a few things right off the bat that I learned from my business. I found out that there was a huge market for residential cleaning services, much bigger than I had ever dreamed. I found that instead of clients interviewing me, I pretty much interviewed them and was able to pick and choose the clients I wanted to work with. The demand was so large I was turning clients away, which was not necessarily a good business decision, but it was within my life goals. I didn't live in a large metropolitan area either, simply a medium-sized American community with a lot of rural areas around it.

In my three years of business, I only lost one client,and that was because the main breadwinner of the family lost their job and they had to cut their household expenses and now had more free time to clean. That's a pretty good track record for client retention.

2
What Do You Want? Goal Setting

A home cleaning business can either provide full-time income or supplemental income depending on your goals. This should be your first place to start.

Goal setting. I know many of you may be inwardly groaning right now, but if you have no idea where you want to go with your business, you most likely won't go anywhere. Also, there may be a sense of discontent later in the business because it went in a direction where you simply didn't want to go. When your goals are clear you have something to aim for and also know what to turn down and why.

Brainstorming session. Get out paper and pencil or write on your computer if you prefer. Try to set aside all distractions for a while. I'm going to walk you through a series of questions to help you sort through your goals. These will help you determine the direction in which you want to go. Just be brutally honest with yourself in this process as that will make this exercise the most effective tool for you.

During the process of answering these questions, jot down any side notes, thoughts or questions that pop up related to the questions. Just write them down under your answer. You can always go back and research those topics or re-define your goals after getting more information. For now, what you are after is a basic, gut instinct.

1. How much money do you want to make per month?

2. Do you want to physically do the cleaning yourself, have a couple of workers with you or manage a team? Some

combination of this? If so, which combination sounds best to you?

3. How many hours per week do you want to work?

4. Are there any specific cleaning tasks that you hate or refuse to do?

5. Are there any specific cleaning tasks that you love to do?

6. Are you okay with heights and being on a ladder?

7. Do you have any chemical sensitivities?

8. Would you be more interested in cleaning-related specialty niches (more on that later) or general weekly home cleaning?

9. Are there certain types of people that you would prefer to clean for?

10. Are there certain types of people that you would dislike cleaning for?

11. When thinking about the overall running of a business, what tasks would you dislike most?

12. When thinking about the overall running of a business, what tasks would you enjoy the most?

13. Do you plan to have or would you want a business partner or will you operate this business as a sole-proprietor?

14. What are your personal strengths?

15. What are your personal weaknesses?

16. Will you want to provide cleaning supplies or have your clients provide them? (more on this subject later in the book)

17. Will you supply the vacuum and mops or will you use your clients'?

18. Would you want to run a cleaning agency, where you supervise those who do the actual cleaning?

After you've finished this, you have a good base to work with. Keep a journal or keeping adding notes, questions, and thoughts that pop into your mind for the next several weeks. You may find that as you are pondering this, new situations and scenarios may come up. By keeping it all organized in writing in one place, you'll most likely be revisiting this worksheet many times and it will provide you with valuable information.

3
Getting Started

After doing your brainstorming goal session, you've now got a rough sketch of where you want to go. Literally think of it as an outline. As you do more research and gain more knowledge, you'll be filling in the blanks. You'll also be making adjustments based on reality and what's available.

Choose a business name. Sometimes this process takes longer than anticipated. Enlist some ideas from friends and family to help. Once you decide on a name, do a quick search to see if that name is already a registered business in your state. You won't want to duplicate another business's name.

Visit a tax accountant or CPA. Find out what exactly you need in your state for record-keeping, mileage, etc. Ask if there are any requirements on your part to get tax deductions on your home expenses if you run an office out of your home. In this portion of preparation, do your best to also get a total overhead cost, so you know what you need to pass on to cover basic expenses.

You will also want to see if it is in your best interest to register your business as a sole owner, a corporation or some other entity.

If you plan to hire employees, now is also the time to ask about payroll taxes, social security, and all the financial aspects of having employees. It also includes setting up who will take care of preparing payroll and payroll expenses, and who will do the financial record-keeping for the business.

If you choose to do it yourself, the tax accountant can assist you in getting everything properly set up and make sure you are in legal compliance on the financial end.

You will also need to open up a business banking account. You will want an account that is totally separate from your personal account.

Once you've decided this is what you are going to do, you'll want to get a business license. Most can be completed online through a simple process for under $50.00. Do an internet search for getting a business license in your town or city, and you'll find information about your state or county's proper governmental licensing requirements. It usually only takes a few minutes.

You'll likely want to get insured or bonded for your business. In a cleaning business, accidents do happen, and you want to be able to compensate your clients when they do occur,plus give them a greater sense of security when hiring you. It also increases your professionalism. Contact local insurance agencies for price quotes on liability insurance for home cleaning businesses. An experienced agent will have recommendations as to how much coverage should be adequate. It's also important if you hire employees to cover your clients in the event that an employee steals from them.

Check out the Small Business Administration as well at: http://www.sba.gov. There are amazing resources there for small businesses including leads on funding sources and other startup help. You may qualify for grants or loans for startup money as well.

You will also want to look at possibly getting a website built, a logo designed, making fliers or brochures, and business cards. If you have a college nearby, sometimes you can either hire graphic design students to help with this or you can approach an instructor to ask if your business perhaps, could be assigned as a class project.   Another valuable resource to get professional quality work done on a budget is to check out http://www.fiverr.com/. This is a site where you can hire people to do many of the above tasks for $5.00 or slightly more, depending on what you need.

4
Cleaning Products

I'm putting this section about cleaning products ahead of pricing as there are some decisions you will need to make concerning this topic before you can move into pricing structures.

A large decision of your cleaning business is whether or not you will supply the cleaning products you will use in a client's home.

There is a general business concept that "the customer is always right." With that said, if a customer has a strong preference in this area, you may want to go with their preference or risk losing that client. Some people have strong feelings about cleaning products especially some who want only organic, non-toxic cleaning products used. Perhaps some may have allergies to certain chemicals or strongly dislike a certain odor. Usually, they will have their own favorite products.

If this is the case, one conversation you might have to have upfront is that you are very willing to use their chosen products, but they should realize that those products might not work as thoroughly and efficiently as the ones you normally work with. As long as you both understand that situation and are agreeable to it, there shouldn't be a problem.

I am biased on this issue. I chose to provide the cleaning products for my clients and I'll tell you my reasoning, but ultimately it really is your decision.

I found some cleaning products made by those working in the house cleaning industry intended for people working in the industry. I'll reveal those favorites at the end of the chapter. I'm not making any kind of commission or referral income from sharing these products with you, I'm simply sharing them because they flat out worked. I found they were economical to use (many I bought full strength and diluted with water per the instructions), but best of all, they were super effective, worked quickly, and made my work look awesome.

Time is money and if you are using inferior products they may take longer to work, you have to work harder physically (more elbow grease), and the results are often less than desirable. When you have a great product that really works, when your client comes home and is wowed by a superb cleaning, especially one they knew they couldn't get on their own with what they normally use, you'll have a faithful and happy client. You'll also have a client who tells their friends and relatives about your service. There's no better marketing than happy, word-of-mouth referrals.

You also don't run the risk of the client either forgetting to buy cleaning supplies or of running out in the middle of a job.

You also do not have to read directions for various products (time waster, but necessary), as you will become very familiar with the products you use consistently and the results you can expect from them.

It's a selling point to potential clients that because you provide the cleaning products, they no longer need to buy their own supplies. You will; however, be setting your prices to reflect that you provide products, but since you will get them at economical prices, it will ultimately save your clients money.

You will also need to decide if you want to supply your own vacuum cleaner and mops or use the clients'. I opted for bringing my own for many of the same reasons listed above for products. Some clients owned poor-quality vacuum machines and I was constantly having to learn new machines (time waster).

As for mops, I needed one that had a large surface so I could cover a lot of square footage quickly. If you get stuck using a swiffer or other small-headed mop, you could easily double, triple or even quadruple the time it takes to complete the floor. You must really focus on the fact that in this business, time IS money, and while you want to do an amazing job, you also want to avoid needless time wasters and shoot for the most efficient routes possible.

Now for product recommendations. Again, these are simply tools and products I found very effective and efficient in my own cleaning business, and I am not making referrals or commissions by passing this info along.

The first recommendation is a book called *Speed Cleaning* on Amazon.com. I know it is sort of strange to read a book about cleaning methods, but I actually learned a lot from this book. It has very practical cleaning tips. I found that I learned about items that I never really thought about before, and the book exposed "blind spots" we most likely all have in cleaning. There is a rhythm and methodology that can not only make your cleaning skills better and more honed, but faster too. However, listen to your body and do not push beyond what you can and should do. You don't want injuries, trust me.

Most of the products I used actually came from the company "The Clean Team http://www.thecleanteam.com/", which wrote the above book, and you can order these products from them. I'll highlight some of my favorite products. Once you get your tax paperwork lined up, you can also order wholesale through them.

Tile Juice - This product was my favorite! Be sure to read the instructions thoroughly; however, on what bathroom surfaces it can be used on, and follow the directions exactly. It cleans bathrooms through chemical action instead of elbow grease. It would get rid of really tough stains that nothing else worked on. I saw old bathtubs and showers that look like new again. I also used their Speed Eraser with the handle for this project.

I found the first time I cleaned a client's home, I really focused on getting the shower and tub area clean from built-up scum and water deposits. This first-time cleaning took longer than normal (tell the client this and allocate time for it), but it was a real "wow" factor for them. I found that I didn't have to use Tile Juice every week once I got it really clean the first time. I used either a Soft Scrub with bleach-type product or similar in between cleanings with Tile Juice.

Red Juice - This is a concentrated, general surface cleaner that you mix into a spray bottle with water. It is very economical to use and works great. It's similar to a 409-type product; it's great on countertops, toilets, appliances, etc.

Blue Juice - This product is a concentrated formula you also mix with water into a spray bottle and is very economical. It's a glass cleaner.

They've got a mop called a Shh-Mop that's fantastic with a large head to cover a lot of square footage quickly. It also has removable covers that you throw into the washer when dirty. You are not dealing with dirty water or spreading dirty water onto floor surfaces. I did use the Shh-mop floor cleaner product for mopping, and it worked great. Be sure to stock up on plenty of the removable wipes even though you will be using many per day.

Pumice stones are wonderful for removing hard water rings in the toilet bowl that simply won't come out any other way. It basically sands them off.

Their cleaning apron will save you many hours of walking back and forth for various supplies. Count it as a necessary time saver!

I used their 100% cotton towels for cleaning rags. They provided dust and lint-free cleaning without streaks for nearly everything. Stock up on these. I used many per household, then just washed them when done. Buy lots. Be sure to wash them a few times before using them; however, to help break them in so they are a bit more absorbent.

When I finished cleaning a bathroom, I sprayed all surfaces, doorknobs, and toilet handles with Lysol or some type of disinfectant spray then wipe down all the surfaces (toilet last) with one of these clean, dry cloths so each surface was dry, sparkling, shiny and free of any stray hairs. Nothing screams that a bathroom is not clean like stray hairs left behind.

Be sure to keep any of these cloths that you may use with furniture polish and waxes completely separate from cloths you use for windows, mirrors, and other cleaning, including the laundry. You don't want those waxes to ruin the other batch of cloths.

The stainless steel cleaner was great for stainless steel appliances and sinks.

Furniture feeder was an amazing product for wood furniture and cabinets. It removed old buildup of waxes, grease and dirt, and also put down a new coat of premium wax that could be buffed into a beautiful shine, which would both moisturize fine wood and protect it.

I loved their genuine ostrich feather duster. It was super soft and gathered dust very well. Feather dusting is for quick, light dusting. When dust is heavy and thick, it is best to use an appropriate cleaner or wax with a cleaning cloth to really wipe up the dirt buildup. The Clean Team also carries a high-quality furniture polish.

I used bleach in toilets and sprayed Lysol on bathroom surfaces before wiping down, so they were disinfected. A good-quality, super-soft squeegee is also a must-have. Don't skimp on quality as the cheap ones are brittle, leave streaks, and smears on glass and mirrors. I also used razor blade scrapers frequently, as well as big toothbrushes for scrubbing in crevices, corners and creases along sinks and tubs.

A few years after, I closed my home cleaning business, occasionally I would run into clients I had or they would call me to ask if I had reconsidered cleaning again or had referrals for other cleaners. I consistently heard the same remarks, "you were the best house cleaner we ever had," "nobody gets our home as clean as you did." I credit these amazing comments to a few things listed above:

Tile juice

Reading the book recommended above and really learning to pay thorough attention to details in cleaning and removing my "blind spots"

Wiping down bathrooms when clean with clean 100% cotton cloths (above) to ensure bathrooms are shiny and dry with no hair left behind.

5
Pricing Structures

Pricing structure is a complicated issue. If you ask 20 different house cleaning businesses how they structure their pricing, you'll likely get 20 different answers.

Many businesses will quote a bid for a set job such as cleaning so many square feet of residential property. Some quote based on a room or the square footage of a room. If that model appeals to you and you can get your figures to work, great.

Personally, I am not a fan of that model, perhaps partly because I'm not strong at guessing how long it will take me to clean a particular room or home until I've done it a couple of times.

I've also found that there are so many variables in housecleaning, I ended up shortchanging either myself or my client. I went to an hourly rate structure. I'll list some reasons why I prefer that mode.

1. Clutter in a home is a huge variable. A home that has lots of clutter to be moved or to clean around takes a far greater amount of time than a home with no clutter.

2. Client expectations of what was "normal weekly cleaning" varied greatly. Some clients truly only wanted the basics, while others wanted lots of extras. With an hourly rate, no problem with the clients who wanted all the extras, they were paying for them. They were happy to get all the extras done, and I was fine with the situation as I was being paid for the time I spent doing it all.

3. It was a more accurate work and time split for both client and business owner. It kept one party from taking

advantage of the other.

If you end up either expanding your home cleaning business or start out with other employees, you may want to get some professional advice on setting prices and employee salaries. In general, consider paying the top dollar you can afford to your employees. You want hardworking, honest, and loyal individuals whom you train to clean to your standards. Employees that will stay, be reliable, and make your company look good are valuable and need to be compensated fairly for that.

You don't want a high turnover rate, ex-employees taking your clients for themselves, doing sloppy work, not showing up, etc. When employees are paid well, it's generally a win-win situation for all concerned. They will see the benefit of working for you and not having to deal with administrative, marketing, and other tasks related to running a business rather than launching a competing business against you. You'll also make some income by doing those tasks on their behalf and grow a bigger business. It may be a business that you grow and someday sell.

Also try to find out what other housecleaners in your area are charging to have a general sense of what your competitors are charging. When I recently did a search, I found a national statistic that indicated an hourly rate from $25 - $35 per hour in United States was the average for 2013. Certainly there will be other factors, such as what your particular market will bear, what your competition is charging, if you live in a more rural area or a large city, and the local economy in general.

If you are a one-person operation, don't wait until you are completely booked to decide what the next step of your business should be. Do that when you are about 80% booked, otherwise you won't have the time to deal with expansion issues, should you want to expand.

It's a good practice to revisit your original goal worksheet every year. You may choose to re-adjust your business based on your original goals or you might have new goals in mind that need to be updated, but either way it will provide valuable insight.

6

Starting with New Clients

Okay, you've got your first potential client calling you and asking about your services and what you charge. What now?

Others may offer other recommendations, but here are mine, which are based upon my experiences. Instead of insisting on listing everything you do and don't do, wasting your time and theirs, start asking them questions based on their needs, such as:

1. What are you looking for in a cleaning service?

2. How frequently?

3. What tasks are you looking to have done?

4. What are you thinking about in terms of potential scheduling? Are certain days better than others or certain times? Sometimes they will only have a particular slot available, and you may already be booked with a regular client at that time. It's a time waster to go through everything only to find at the end of the process that you can't make scheduling work.

Ask to meet with the client for a detailed walk through at their home to discuss specific tasks that they want completed and any special instructions that may be needed, so that you can provide an accurate quote for your services.

Here's where it may get a bit tricky. Do not give price quotes over the phone!. Just state that it is your company's policy to give a quote in person as there are just too many variables involved to give accurate pricing otherwise. It's also a time for you to provide references to the client, answer any questions they may have about you or your business, and to see if you are a good fit for their situation and vice versa.

Early on in my business, I made exemptions to that guideline and every time, I regretted it big time! I also found that the people who really balked at meeting me for an in-person meeting ended up being trouble. Think of it as a red flag. With every one of those, I ended up canceling their services because they were too troublesome to be worth the effort.

In general, I found those who demanded price quotes over the phone were simply going through the phonebook looking for the cheapest service. Generally, they were also the ones who wanted me to do the most and were the pickiest, of course at a bargain basement pricing. If that's your cup of tea for a clientele, go for it, but for me, no thanks. There were too many truly wonderful clients out there who were gladly willing to pay a fair price for a quality service, and very appreciative of your work.

One of the cases that was a disaster was willing to meet me for a price quote and walk through. However, it was one week before a holiday and she had guests arriving shortly, and she literally begged me to do at least do 3 hours of cleaning while I was there too. I normally would not do this as I am also interviewing the client as well, but it was the holidays, I had the time and I fell to her pleading. The house was a total disaster—not just clutter and normal dirt from life, but truly filthy. There were human feces spread on the walls in the bathrooms and other bio-hazardous conditions. There was a male renter who lived upstairs who gawked at me the whole time I was bent over the bathtub scrubbing, then made a pass at me. Because I had given my word to work for 3 hours over the phone, I felt obligated to keep my word. Had I only stuck to my policy of a walk-through / interview process first, I would never have agreed to even a three-hour job.

You would think that one terrible experience would have been enough for me to learn my lesson, but in another situation I gave in as well to a cleaning time during the interview meeting. Perhaps I thought the above situation was just a fluke, perhaps I was in denial or simply desperate for more clients, but I tried again. I went with trepidation and it was equally as bad, just different circumstances. I literally had to just get home as quickly as possible afterwards to shower. I will spare you the details on what I encountered there. Suffice it to say, I didn't accept the job. Never again, even if it meant losing a potential good client.

When I first began a home cleaning business, I assumed that most of my clients would be double income, working adults, in the home who simply didn't have time to clean. While many did fit into that category, what surprised me was that a large percentage of my clientele ended up being healthy elderly singles and couples. Most of them had very neat and tidy homes, but simply needed someone on a weekly or bi-weekly basis to come in and do the big stuff: floors, mopping, dusting, and scrubbing out the bathrooms.

When you go to do your price quote / walk-through interview, think of it as a mutual interview. You are there to interview them as much as they are interviewing you. This is a time to give them your references (I'll go more into how to get those when you are brand new in the marketing section), your business cards, and answering any questions they have about you and your business. It's the time to explain any policies you may have and discuss their needs.

It is a good idea to draft up a simple form for your use when doing a walk-through. Keep it simple, have a sheet dedicated to kitchen, bathrooms, living room, bedrooms, and other. Put down on your basic form checkboxes like vacuuming, dusting, mopping, scrubbing tubs, showers, toilets & sinks, wipe down counters, mirrors, changing sheets, doing laundry, making beds, and any other normal tasks that come to mind.

As you walk through room by room with a client, ask a lot of questions. The most knowledge you gain, the better you'll be able to do a job that pleases the client. It is very important at this stage to determine their definition of what a weekly or bi-weekly cleaning job entails. This varies greatly from person to person. For some, it really is the tasks listed above. For others, it also includes cleaning the cat litter box, vacuuming, sweeping the front porch, doing dishes or any other task they want done.

Ask about how they want clutter dealt with. Will they have cleared the whole house before your arrival? Do they want you to put it in a central location? Leave it alone? Write notes on your sheet as you go for everything they comment on.

I then give an estimate for how long I think it will take me to do the job and the price (including providing products). I tell them that the first few times, it really is a rough estimate of time until I get in there cleaning and find more accurately how long it takes to do their home. Generally, the first few times it also takes longer because you're doing some deeper cleaning in the bathroom for water and soap buildup, and after it's gone; regular maintenance cleaning goes faster. Ask them their preference at this point: if it's okay to do longer cleaning sessions the first one to three times (which cost more) or if they prefer you do as much as you can in the set amount of hours they indicate they want. Tell them that after the first one to three times, you can discuss together what's best with regards to accurate time for weekly maintenance cleaning. It's also the time they will discover other items they will want you to either do or not do in going forward.

Usually these are items that they never thought about before or simply overlooked. Think of it as fine-tuning the service to their individual needs. This is a normal process. Explain this process to them before you even start and stress the need for open communication, so that you can provide the best service possible for them.

If at this point it was a job I felt like I wanted to take on, I would ask the client if they would like to book a cleaning appointment. If they do, book the appointment and discuss how to get in. Some will give you a key, some are home when you are there, some will hide a key; it's totally up to their discretion.

If they are not ready to book the appointment, graciously hand them your card, and ask them to call to set up an appointment when they've made a decision or feel ready. Sending a short thank you note for their time and meeting with you is a nice gesture.

If it wasn't a client I was willing to take on, I either told them up front I didn't think we would be a good fit together or said my availability was currently booked, I would put them on a waiting list, and get back to them if openings came up. It's up to you how you wish to decline a job.

It's important to get your discussion in writing in some way for both of you before starting the job. Some companies go with a formal contract. I wanted something a little more like a handshake with friendlier terms. It's up to you how you want to proceed with this step. I sent the client an email (and informed them I would be doing so for their approval) outlining the notes I just took: the tasks they wanted, the amount of time they wanted and any other thing that was mentioned, gave the pay quote, and reminded them that payment was due upon completion of each cleaning job. I then asked the client to look over the email to verify its accuracy or to clarify anything that didn't seem correct or if they had questions. I asked them to respond to the email once it looked acceptable to them, printed it, and made a file for that client. Then we had a record of terms before work was started. I found that this process worked well for my business model.

Be willing to hear your clients out if they're asking for exceptions. I had one client referred to me by another client, but she lived 45-minutes away in a town I had no intention of covering. She so wanted my services, she offered to pay not only my gas costs, but also my regular hourly rate for drive time both ways. Needless to say, I took that job, and it was a good one.

Finally, find something that is an extra touch that sets your company apart from your competition. Underpromise and overdeliver. Perhaps it's leaving a little mint on their pillows like hotels do, maybe it's a note wishing them a nice day, perhaps a flower; a small gesture that says you value them and their business. Send the new weekly client a personal thank you card thanking them for their business. These small details make a huge difference in your business!

7
Marketing Ideas & Strategies

Always put yourself in the shoes of your clients. It's vulnerable to allow a total stranger to come into your home, possibly when you're not even there, to clean. Perhaps they've given you a key to their home and alarm codes. Its important to take every step necessary to earn their trust, guard their trust, and take care of their home and possessions.

Getting properly licensed and bonded is also part of that assurance process. It's also critical to get several good references in writing that can also be verified by phone if necessary as to your work and your character.

When you are first opening a new business that can be difficult, but here's a couple of ideas. Think of some people in your community who may be community leaders or hold jobs of high reputation like doctors, nurses, teachers, prominent business people, etc. If you personally don't know of anyone, ask people you do know, if they know of any. Contact that person and tell them that you are opening a home cleaning business and are seeking some startup referrals for potential clients. Ask if you could do a couple hour cleaning job for them for free, in exchange for a written reference if they like your work. Do this and get it in writing, preferably on their business letterhead with their signature. If you feel comfortable with the situation afterwards, ask if they might be willing to occasionally take a phone call if a potential client is trying to verify that the referral is legitimate. Some won't be willing, simply due to time. Make copies of these referrals and give them to all of your potential clients. Some of these free jobs might even become customers after they see your work or maybe willing to pass your business cards on to their acquaintances.

Ask for character referrals from people you have known well for many years. In their letters, have them state how long they've known you, the nature of the relationship, why they think you'd do a great job, and make an excellent house cleaner for them. You especially want them to vouch for your honesty.

It's also a good idea to order a fingerprinted, FBI background check on yourself to provide to your clients. It's fairly simple to do and the cost is minimal. Here's a link for more information on that: http://www.fbi.gov/about-us/cjis/criminal-history-summary-checks. It's a wonderful thing to provide a copy of this to potential clients. If you hire employees, it's important to have background checks run on them as well.

Word-of-mouth will be your most effective advertising and marketing strategy, but that takes time to build. At first, you will need to do some marketing to get those first clients.

Depending on the type of clients you want to try to market to, you'll want to target your marketing there. For instance, if you want to do a new construction building cleaning, you would want to target contractors and real estate agents.

You may want to either build a website or have one built for you. Consider having your town or city in the domain name to help it appear in more local searches. Fiverr.com can be a great resource for technical help on a budget. You could also do some paid Google ads with your website, specifically targeting only your local area for those seeking house cleaning services.

A small classified ad in a local newspaper can be very effective too. Putting up fliers near senior housing areas or senior citizen centers can be good.

You may want to also submit a press release to your local paper about the startup of your business, which can be a great way to get free exposure and new customers.

You can try posting your services on Craigslist for free. Network with the local Chamber of Commerce members and any other business networking groups that may be in your area. It all starts with relationships.

Another idea (after reading the last chapter) is putting together introductory special cleaning packages and running a sales promotion in the local newspaper with the goal of trying to convert some of those to regular weekly cleaning jobs. The weekly cleaning jobs are the bread and butter of the business, and should be a fairly high priority for services.

Once you do land a client or two, you can give them special referral discounts or some other incentive for every client they refer to you.

8
To Specialize or Not?

This last section is another one to inspire brainstorming and perhaps ideas you hadn't thought of before. In fact, after reading it, you may want to do more goal-setting, notetaking or further research into some of it.

Some people, when opening up a cleaning service, are open to take just about any cleaning jobs that come their way, and that's great. That is more of a generalist. Others prefer to specialize in one type of cleaning service, as there are so many out there. Below I'm going to list a lot of areas that could be launched as specialized services.

Residential weekly or bi-weekly home cleaning services

Business office cleaning services - would most likely entail mostly nights or weekend work.

New construction cleaning - getting off tape, stickers, drywall mud, dried paint, etc. from windows, tubs and general cleaning to get a place move-in ready. Target would most likely be contractors and real estate agents.

Apartment move in and out prep - some apartment complexes hire cleaning services to ready vacant apartments for their next tenants. This could also include tenants who want to get the cleaning done so they can get their full deposit back. This service could also include property management businesses preparing for a new tenant in condo or home rentals.

Crime scene cleaning - this one is a bit "out there," and not everyone can do it. You would need to do much research on handling human bio-hazard cleaning. Find if the police departments even has a market for it in your local area is important.

Childcare and daycare cleaning services - This would involve effective disinfecting of toys and other surfaces in a manner that is safe for children, perhaps even if there are hard surface floors using steam cleaners that sterilize floors. Most likely, this would involve cleaning during off hours.

Special Packages

This section I'll call "special packages." Each one could be made into an either stand-alone, specialized business or marketed as a specialty package you could offer your regular clients at additional cost. They could also be marketed with special sales or promotions in order to gain more regular weekly clients if they like your services.

Cleaning appliances, large and small - deep cleaning refrigerators, ovens, washers, dryers, microwaves, blenders, mixers, etc. This might involve vacuuming the back of refrigerator coils, and changing filters if some appliances have filters. It should involve both the inside and outside of the appliances.

Carpets & hard floor cleaning - disinfecting hard floor surfaces with steam cleaners and carpet shampooing. This could also include upholstery cleaning of furniture.

Inside cabinets, closets, and reorganizing - Most people's cabinets and drawer interiors are a mess. This service could include removing everything, cleaning the interiors ,and perhaps laying down drawer liners, tossing out old, expired and unused items, then re-organizing and putting everything else back. Organizing systems could be developed as well.

Cleaning mini-blinds, drapes, curtains, and / or window cleaning - Even if the drape and curtain cleaning was simply taking them down to the local dry cleaner, then re-hanging, this could be an amazing service for everything to do with windows. You would have to consider; however, if you wanted to do outside, higher than one-story windows,and how to access them safely or if that was off-limits for your service.

Deep cleaning wood furniture and cabinets - The product in an earlier chapter called "Furniture Feeder" would be ideal to use in this type of business. It can be used on all wood surfaces including fine wood furniture. It strips and cleans off old wax buildup, dirt, grease, and grime. You then buff and polish on a coat of superb carnauba wax. It both provides luster and sheen for wood and moisturizes and protects wood.

Polishing metals around the house including silver, copper, and brass - These might be silverware, light fixtures, doorknobs, chandeliers, lamps, and/or decorative items in the home. These surfaces usually tarnish and get dull with time and do not usually get much cleaning attention. Occasional polishing with proper products can add a surprisingly big difference to a room.

Deep cleaning of pots & pans - This is often an overlooked area of thorough cleaning in a home: going through the kitchen and really scrubbing and polishing pots, pans and other bake ware. It could also include re-seasoning any cast iron cookware.

Starting a home cleaning business can be a very rewarding and profitable endeavor. There are so many options that can be tailored to your goals. I hope this book has inspired ideas and possibilities for you.

If you enjoyed this book or received value from it in any way, would you be kind enough to leave a review for this book on Amazon? I would be so grateful. Thank you!

Made in the USA
Lexington, KY
20 June 2016